PESCATARIAN COOKBOOK

MAIN COURSE - Breakfast, Main Course, Dessert and Snacks recipes

TABLE OF CONTENTS

Introduction

Pescatarian recipes for personal enjoyment but also for family enjoyment. You will love them for sure for how easy it is to prepare them.

TUNA AVOCADO BOWL

Serves: **2**

Prep Time: **5**   Minutes

Cook Time: **10**   Minutes

Total Time: **15**   Minutes

INGREDIENTS

- 1 can tuna
- ¼ celery stalk
- ¼ tsp mustard
- ½ lemon
- ¼ shallot
- 1 tablespoon parsley
- 1 tablespoon mayonnaise
- ¼ tablespoon black pepper
- 2 avocados

DIRECTIONS

1. In a bowl place all ingredients, except the avocados, and mix well

2. Cut avocados in half and scoop out some of the avocado flesh

3. Spoon the tuna mixture into the avocados

4. When ready serve or refrigerate

Serves: *2*
Prep Time: *10*   Minutes

Cook Time: *15*   Minutes

Total Time: *25*   Minutes

INGREDIENTS

- 1 avocado
- ¼ lemon
- 2 eggs
- Pinch of salt
- Pinch of black pepper

DIRECTIONS

1. Cut the avocado in half and scoop out some of the avocado flesh
2. Squeeze over lemon juice
3. Crack your eggs into the each of the avocado half
4. Place on a baking tray and bake for 12-15 minutes at 450 F
5. When ready remove and serve

Serves: **2**

Prep Time: **5** Minutes

Cook Time: **5** Minutes

Total Time: **10** Minutes

INGREDIENTS

- 1 avocado
- 150 g mushrooms
- 1 tablespoon olive oil
- 2 slices sour dough bread
- Pinch of salt

DIRECTIONS

1. In a frying pan add the mushrooms and a pinch of salt, cook for 3-4 minutes
2. Toast bread and place on a plate
3. Add avocado slices, mushrooms and serve

Serves: **6**

Prep Time: **10**   Minutes

Cook Time: **25**   Minutes

Total Time: **35**   Minutes

INGREDIENTS

- 1 shallot
- ¼ red pepper
- ¼ green pepper
- 2 oz tomatoes
- ¼ tsp paprika
- 4 eggs

DIRECTIONS

1. In a frying pan add the shallot, tomatoes, paprika, green pepper and red pepper
2. Cook for 8-10 minutes or until soft
3. In a bowl beat 4 eggs and add the contents of your frying pan to the bowl
4. Mix well and spoon the ingredients into a muffin tray and bake at 400 F for 12-15 minutes, serve when ready

Serves: **6**

Prep Time: **10** Minutes

Cook Time: **25** Minutes

Total Time: **35** Minutes

INGREDIENTS

- ¼ onion
- 2 oz. mushrooms
- 1 garlic clove
- 4 eggs
- 2 oz. smoked salmon
- salt

DIRECTIONS

1. In a frying pan add mushrooms, onion, garlic and salt, cook for 5-6 minutes or until soft
2. In a bowl beat 4 eggs, then add contents of the frying pan and smoked salmon
3. Pour the mixture into a muffin tray
4. Bake at 400 F for 12-15 minutes
5. When ready remove and serve

Serves: **4**

Prep Time: **5** Minutes

Cook Time: **10** Minutes

Total Time: **15** Minutes

INGREDIENTS

- 1 oz. brown sugar
- 100g self-rising flour
- 1 egg
- 120 ml milk
- ¼ lemon rind
- Butter
- ½ banana

DIRECTIONS

1. In a bowl combine all ingredients together, except the butter
2. In a frying pan add butter and heat well
3. Pour ¼ batter and cook for 2-3 minutes per side
4. When ready remove and serve

Serves: **2**

Prep Time: **5**   Minutes

Cook Time: **10**   Minutes

Total Time: **15**   Minutes

INGREDIENTS

- 1 avocado
- ¼ cup red onion
- 1 tomato
- ¼ green chili pepper
- 1 tablespoon cilantro
- 1 tsp cumin
- ¼ tsp salt
- ¼ tsp black pepper
- ¼ lime
- 2 slices bread
- 2 oz. cheddar cheese

DIRECTIONS

1. In a bowl mash avocado, add green chili peppers, cilantro, cumin, salt, lime juice, tomato and mix well
2. Toast bread slices and spoon guacamole over the bread
3. Cover with cheese and another bread slice and broil in the over for 4-5 minutes or until cheese is melted
4. When ready remove and serve

Serves: **3**

Prep Time: **5**   Minutes

Cook Time: **10**   Minutes

Total Time: **15**   Minutes

INGREDIENTS

- 2 avocados
- ¼ red onion
- 1 green chili pepper
- Handful of cilantros
- 1 tomato
- 1 tsp cumin
- Juice of ½ lime
- 1 cucumber

DIRECTIONS

1. In a bowl mash the avocado, add onion, tomato, salt, cumin, pepper and lime juice
2. Cut the cucumbers into 3-4-inch slices and spoon some out the flesh
3. Fill each cup with guacamole and serve

Serves: **4**

Prep Time: **5**   Minutes

Cook Time: **10**   Minutes

Total Time: **15**   Minutes

INGREDIENTS

- 2 avocados
- ¼ onion
- 1 green chili pepper
- ¼ tsp salt
- Handful of cilantros
- 1 tsp cumin
- Juice of ½ lime
- 1 tomato

Quesadillas

- 1 tablespoon olive oil
- 4 tortillas
- 2 oz. vegetarian cheese

DIRECTIONS

1. In a bowl combine all ingredients for guacamole mix well and set aside
2. In a pan place each tortilla with cheese and cook on low heat until cheese is melted
3. When the cheese is melted add guacamole and wrap the tortilla
4. When ready remove from heat and cut the quesadillas and serve

Serves: **4**

Prep Time: **10**   Minutes

Cook Time: **30**   Minutes

Total Time: **40**   Minutes

INGREDIENTS

- 8-10 sardine fillets
- 2 tablespoons olive oil
- 2 tablespoons lemon juice
- 2 garlic cloves
- ¼ tablespoon parsley
- Bread slices

DIRECTIONS

1. In a bowl combine lemon juice and olive oil
2. Brush each sardine fillet with lemon mixture
3. Place sardine fillet in a saucepan and fry for 1-2 minutes per side, add garlic and chili and fry for 2-3 minutes
4. Toast 2-3 bread slices and place salmon fillets and serve with parsley

Serves: **6**

Prep Time: **5**   Minutes

Cook Time: **10**   Minutes

Total Time: **15**   Minutes

INGREDIENTS

- 1 lb. carrots
- 2 cloves garlic
- 2 tablespoons olive oil
- 2 cucumbers
- 1 tsp cumin
- 1 tsp coriander
- 1 tsp honey
- ¼ tsp black pepper
- ¼ tsp salt
- 2 tablespoons lemon juice

DIRECTIONS

1. **Place the garlic and carrots on a baking tray and bake at 375F for 12-15 minutes**

2. Cut cucumber into 3-4-inch slices and scoop some of the fresh

3. In a blender add garlic, carrots and remaining ingredients and blend until smooth

4. When ready spoon into cucumber slices and serve

Serves: **8**

Prep Time: **10** Minutes

Cook Time: **30** Minutes

Total Time: **40** Minutes

INGREDIENTS

- 2 cups oats
- 2 tablespoons protein powder
- 1 tsp cocoa powder
- 1 tsp nutmeg
- 1 tablespoon sesame seeds
- 2 tablespoons peanut butter
- 1 tablespoon honey
- 1 cup chocolate chips

DIRECTIONS

1. In a bowl combine sesame seeds, oats, cocoa powder, protein powder, nutmeg and mix well
2. Add in peanut butter, honey, chocolate chips and mix well

3. Shape 8-10 balls and place refrigerate for 30-45 minutes

4. When ready remove and serve

Serves: **2**

Prep Time: **5**   Minutes

Cook Time: **5**   Minutes

Total Time: **10**   Minutes

INGREDIENTS

- ½ lb. smoked mackerel
- 2 sprig onion
- 1 sprig dill
- 1 oz. cress
- Juice of ½ lemon
- 100g cream cheese
- ¼ tsp mustard
- ¼ tsp salt

DIRECTIONS

1. In a bowl add mackerel and mash well
2. Add onions, cress, dill and mix well
3. Add zest, lemon juice, cream cheese, mustard and mix well
4. When ready serve on toast bread

Serves: **4**

Prep Time: **10** Minutes

Cook Time: **30** Minutes

Total Time: **40** Minutes

INGREDIENTS

- 200 g smoked salmon
- 150g cream cheese
- 2 oz. double cream
- ¼ tablespoon lemon juice
- 1 tsp dill
- 1 tsp chives
- ¼ tsp salt

DIRECTIONS

1. In a blender add smoked salmon and the rest of the ingredients
2. Blend until smooth
3. When ready serve on toast bread and garnish with dill

Serves: **2**

Prep Time: **5**   Minutes

Cook Time: **5**   Minutes

Total Time: **10**   Minutes

INGREDIENTS

- 2 tablespoons unsalted butter
- 1 cup onion
- 6 eggs
- Salt
- 4 oz. vegetarian cheese

DIRECTIONS

1. In a bowl beat eggs with onion and salt
2. In a frying pan melt butter and pour eggs
3. Add grated vegetarian cheese over
4. Cook for 4-5 minutes
5. When ready remove and serve

Serves: *2*

Prep Time: *5*   Minutes

Cook Time: *5*   Minutes

Total Time: *10* Minutes

INGREDIENTS

- 2 tablespoons unsalted butter
- 2 cloves garlic
- 4 anchovy filets

DIRECTIONS

1. In a saucepan melt butter
2. Stir in anchovies and garlic
3. Cook for 4-5 minutes and cover with a lid
4. Place popcorn in a bowl and serve

Serves: **2**

Prep Time: **5**   Minutes

Cook Time: **5**   Minutes

Total Time: **10**   Minutes

INGREDIENTS

- 2 bread slices
- 1 cup homemade bean pate
- 1 avocado

DIRECTIONS

1. Toast 2 bread slices
2. Cut avocado into thin slices
3. Spread homemade bean pate over toast and top with avocado slices
4. Sprinkle salt and serve

Serves: *1*

Prep Time: *5*   Minutes

Cook Time: *5*   Minutes

Total Time: *10*   Minutes

INGREDIENTS

- ¼ cup brewed coffee
- ½ cup soy milk
- ¼ cup hazelnuts
- 1 cup ice cubes
- Coconut flakes

DIRECTIONS

1. In a blender add all ingredients and blend until smooth
2. Pour the smoothie in glass and serve

Serves: *1*

Prep Time: *5*   Minutes

Cook Time: *10*   Minutes

Total Time: *15*   Minutes

INGREDIENTS

- 4 eggs
- ¼ tsp salt

DIRECTIONS

1. In a pot bring water to a bowl
2. Break the 4 eggs into boiling water and let them simmer for 10 minutes
3. When ready remove and serve

Serves: *1*
Prep Time: *5*   Minutes

Cook Time: *5*   Minutes

Total Time: *10* Minutes

INGREDIENTS

- 1-pint sweet cherries
- 2 tablespoons honey
- 2 tsp red wine vinegar
- 2 cups ricotta cheese
- Toasted bread
- ½ cup almonds
- min

DIRECTIONS

1. In a bowl toss together honey, cherries and vinegar, season with salt
2. Spoon ricotta cheese into bowls and top with almonds, mint and cherries
3. Serve when ready

SALMON SALAD

Serves: **2**

Prep Time: **5** Minutes

Cook Time: **5** Minutes

Total Time: **10** Minutes

INGREDIENTS

- ¼ cup olive oil
- 2 tablespoons red wine vinegar
- 1 tablespoon lemon juice
- ¼ tsp salt
- ¼ cup water
- 4 oz. cooked salmon
- 2 tomatoes
- 1 cucumber
- ¼ cup olives

DIRECTIONS

1. In a bowl combine all ingredients together
2. Add salad dressing and serve

Serves: **2**

Prep Time: **5** Minutes

Cook Time: **5** Minutes

Total Time: **10** Minutes

INGREDIENTS

- 1 head cauliflower
- 1 tablespoon curry powder
- ¼ cup olive oil
- 1 tsp salt
- 1 cup quinoa
- 1 cup cabbage
- 1 tsp arugula
- 1 cucumber
- 1 cup raisins

DIRECTIONS

1. In a bowl combine all ingredients together
2. Add salad dressing and serve

Serves: *4*
Prep Time: *10*   Minutes

Cook Time: *8*   Hours

Total Time: *8*   Hours

INGREDIENTS

- 2 cups low-sodium vegetable broth
- 1 can diced tomatoes
- 1 onion
- 1 carrot
- 1 celery stalk
- 1 cup green lentils
- 1 tablespoon olive oil
- 1 clove garlic
- 1 tsp tomato paste
- ¼ tsp coriander

DIRECTIONS

1. Place all the ingredients in a slow cook and cook on low for 7-8 hours
2. When ready Ladle into bowls and top with yogurt

Serves: **2**

Prep Time: **5** Minutes

Cook Time: **5** Minutes

Total Time: **10** Minutes

INGREDIENTS

- 1 can tuna
- ¼ red onion
- 1 tablespoon garlic hummus
- 1 tablespoon bbq sauce
- Black pepper
- 2 slices bread
- ¼ avocado

DIRECTIONS

1. In a bowl combine tuna, hummus, onion, bbq sauce and pepper
2. Toast bread and add tuna on both sides
3. Top with avocado slices and onion
4. Serve when ready

Serves: *4*

Prep Time: *10*   Minutes

Cook Time: *30*   Minutes

Total Time: *40*   Minutes

INGREDIENTS

- 2 cans tuna
- 2 celery stalks
- 1 cucumber
- 4 radishes
- 2 onions
- 1 red onion
- ¼ Kalamata olives
- 1 bunch parsley
- 10 mint leaves
- 1 tomato
- 1 serving mustard vinaigrette

DIRECTIONS

1. In a bowl combine all ingredients together
2. Add salad dressing and serve

Serves: **2**

Prep Time: **5** Minutes

Cook Time: **10** Minutes

Total Time: **15** Minutes

INGREDIENTS

- ¼ cup mayonnaise
- 1 tsp lemon
- 1 tsp lime juice
- ¼ cup scallion
- 1 tsp avocado oil
- 1 can tuna
- 2 tortillas

DIRECTIONS

1. In a bowl combine scallion, lemon, lime juice and mayonnaise
2. In a pan sauté tuna
3. Heat tortillas and place tuna mixture onto each tortilla
4. Top with greens, scallion and mayonnaise mixture

Serves: **2**

Prep Time: **5**   Minutes

Cook Time: **5**   Minutes

Total Time: **10** Minutes

INGREDIENTS

- 2 cans tuna
- 1 red bell pepper
- 1 can black beans
- 1 can black olives
- 1 can yellow corn
- 2 tomatoes
- 2 avocados

DRESSING

- ½ cup Greek yogurt
- ¼ cup mayonnaise
- 1 tsp garlic powder
- ¼ tsp cumin

DIRECTIONS

1. In a bowl combine all ingredients together
2. In another bowl combine all ingredients for the dressing
3. Add dressing, mix well and serve

Serves: **2**
Prep Time: **5**   Minutes

Cook Time: **10**   Minutes

Total Time: **15**   Minutes

INGREDIENTS

- ½ cup quinoa
- ½ cup zucchini
- 1 carrot
- 1 can tuna
- ½ cup cabbage
- ½ cup chickpeas
- Cilantro
- Juice of ½ lime

DIRECTIONS

1. In a bowl add quinoa and top with zucchini, cabbage, chickpeas, carrot, onion and tuna
2. Add cilantro on top and lime juice
3. Serve when ready

Serves: **2**

Prep Time: **10**   Minutes

Cook Time: **30**   Minutes

Total Time: **40**   Minutes

INGREDIENTS

- 4 oz. bacon
- 1 onion
- 4 celery stalks
- 2 cloves garlic
- ¼ cup flour
- 2 cups clam juice
- 2 cups water
- 1 sprig thyme
- 1 bay leaf
- 1 lb. potatoes
- 1 cup clams
- 2 cups heavy cream

DIRECTIONS

1. **In a pot add bacon and cook until crisp**

2. Add celery, onion, garlic, flour and cook for another 8-10 minutes

3. Add water, clam juice, potatoes, thyme and bay leaf

4. Bring to a boil and simmer for 15-20 minutes

5. Stir in heavy cream, clams and continue to cook

6. When ready remove from heat and serve with toast

Serves: **2**

Prep Time: **10**   Minutes

Cook Time: **40**   Minutes

Total Time: **50**   Minutes

INGREDIENTS

- 2 beets
- 2 garlic cloves
- 2 tablespoons olive oil
- 2 cups beans
- 1 tablespoon red wine vinegar
- 2 tablespoons crème fraiche
- 8 oz. linguine

DIRECTIONS

1. Place the beet wedges and garlic on a roasting tray and roast at 425 F for 30 minutes or until tender
2. In a blender add roasted beets and blend until smooth
3. Add the rest of the ingredients and blend again
4. When ready serve with cooked linguine

Serves: *4*

Prep Time: *10*   Minutes

Cook Time: *40*   Minutes

Total Time: *50*   Minutes

INGREDIENTS

- 1 can cream of mushroom soup
- ¼ cup milk
- 1 tsp soy sauce
- ¼ tsp black pepper
- 2 cans green beans
- 1 cup onions
- 1 cup mushrooms
- 1 sheet puff pastry
- 1 tablespoon butter

DIRECTIONS

1. Stir the cream of mushrooms soup, black pepper, green beans, milk, soy sauce, 2/3 cup onions and mushrooms in a bowl

2. Spoon mixture into a casserole dish
3. Bake for 30-35 minutes at 425 F
4. Sprinkle with remaining onions and serve

Serves: *4*
Prep Time: *10*   Minutes

Cook Time: *30*   Minutes

Total Time: *40*   Minutes

INGREDIENTS

- 2 purple yams
- 2 tablespoons coconut oil
- 1 tsp tahini
- ¼ lime
- ½ tsp salt

DIRECTIONS

1. Preheat the oven to 375 F
2. Place the yams on a baking sheet and roast for 20-25 minutes
3. Slice the yams in half lengthwise and transfer to a platter
4. Press the yam halves into the plates, add coconut oil, and drizzle tahini, squeeze lime juice and grate the lime zest on top
5. Add salt and serve

Serves: **2**

Prep Time: **10** Minutes

Cook Time: **20** Minutes

Total Time: **30** Minutes

INGREDIENTS

- 2 oz. fish paste
- 150g pasta
- ¼ onion
- 100g yogurt
- 1 bunch parsley
- 1 tablespoon lemon juice

DIRECTIONS

1. In a saucepan bring water to a boil, add pasta and simmer for 10-12 minutes
2. In a frying pan add onion, parsley, lemon juice and cook until onion is soft
3. Add yogurt and fish paste to onion mixture
4. Remove cooked pasta, add onion mixture and serve with parsley

Serves: **6**

Prep Time: **10**   Minutes

Cook Time: **20**   Minutes

Total Time: **30**   Minutes

INGREDIENTS

- 2 eggs
- 200 ml skimmed milk
- 200 g plain flour
- 200 g brioche crumbs
- 4 smoked eels
- Salt

CRÈME FRAICHE DIP

- 200g beetroot
- 2 oz. crème fraiche
- 2 oz. yogurt
- ¼ wine vinegar

DIRECTIONS

1. For crème fraiche place all the ingredients in a blender and blend until smooth

2. For eel mix the eggs and milk together

3. In separate dishes add flour, egg wash and brioche crumbs

4. Roll the eel pieces in the flour and place them into egg wash and them place them into the brioche crumbs

5. Heat oil in a pan and fry until golden brown

6. When ready transfer to a plate and serve with crème fraiche

Serves: *4*

Prep Time: *10*   Minutes

Cook Time: *30*   Minutes

Total Time: *40*   Minutes

INGREDIENTS

- 40 achovy fillets
- 200 ml lemon juice
- 100g wine vinegar
- ¼ tsp salt
- Olive oil
- ¼ tsp Black pepper

DIRECTIONS

1. For the marinate combine wine vinegar, lemon juice and salt
2. Pour the marinate into a bowl
3. Add the anchovies and marinade for 30 minutes
4. Drain the anchovies and place them on a serving plate
5. Drizzle olive and serve

Serves: **2**

Prep Time: **10**   Minutes

Cook Time: **15**   Minutes

Total Time: **25**   Minutes

INGREDIENTS

- 4 cod fillets
- 1 lb. cooked chickpeas
- 2 oz. olive oil
- 100 ml white wine
- 2 garlic cloves
- 2 sprigs of rosemary

DIRECTIONS

1. In a pan pour wine, water and oil and bring to a simmer
2. Add rosemary, cod fillets, garlic and cook for 5-10 minutes
3. Add the chickpeas, salt and cook for 4-5 minutes
4. When ready remove from heat and serve

Serves: **4**

Prep Time: **10** Minutes

Cook Time: **30** Minutes

Total Time: **40** Minutes

INGREDIENTS

- 10-12 scallops
- 1 orange
- 1 garlic clove
- 100g almonds
- 2 tablespoons olive oil
- 1 pinch salt

DIRECTIONS

1. In a bowl mix garlic, olive oil, orange juice and salt
2. Toss the scallops in the marinade and let them chill for 20-30 minutes
3. Place the scallops on a baking tray and sprinkle almonds
4. Bake for 10-15 minutes at 400 F
5. When ready remove from the oven and serve

Serves: *4*

Prep Time: *20*   Minutes

Cook Time: *10*   Minutes

Total Time: *30*   Minutes

INGREDIENTS

- ¾ cup rice
- 2 scallions
- salt
- 2-quarts chicken stock
- 4 slices fresh ginger

DIRECTIONS

1. In a saucepan add rice and cover with water
2. Add ginger, scallion, stock and bring to boil
3. Lower the heat and simmer for 5-10 minutes
4. Cover and cook for one hour
5. Taste and add salt if necessary, before serving

Serves: *4*
Prep Time: *10*   Minutes

Cook Time: *30*   Minutes

Total Time: *40*   Minutes

INGREDIENTS

- 1 red onion
- 2/4 lbs. white fish

MARINADE

- ½ tsp salt
- 1 scallion
- ½ tsp sugar
- 1 tablespoon canola oil
- 1 tablespoon fish sauce
- 2 tablespoons cider vinegar
- 2 tablespoons ginger
- 2 tablespoons cilantro
- 6 cups rice

DIRECTIONS

1. In a bowl mix the following marinade ingredients: ginger, cilantro, salt, sugar, fish sauce, oil and add fish and onion, set aside
2. In a saucepan, bring to boil the rice soup, divide the fish among the soup bowls
3. Garnish with scallion and serve

Serves: **4**

Prep Time: **10** Minutes

Cook Time: **10** Minutes

Total Time: **20** Minutes

INGREDIENTS

- ¼ lbs. noodle
- ¼ lbs. baby spinach
- 3 oz. cooked prawn
- ¼ lbs. snap pea
- 1 carrot

DRESSING

- 1 red chili
- 1 tsp fish sauce
- 1 tablespoon mint
- 2 tablespoons rice vinegar
- 1 tsp sugar

DIRECTIONS

1. **In a bowl add all dressing ingredients and mix well**

2. In another bowl add salad ingredients and mix well, pour dressing over salad and serve

SHRIMP WITH GARLIC

Serves: **4**

Prep Time: **10**   Minutes

Cook Time: **15**   Minutes

Total Time: **25**   Minutes

INGREDIENTS

- 1 lb. shrimp
- ¼ tsp baking soda
- 2 tablespoons oil
- 2 tsp minced garlic
- ¼ cup vermouth
- 2 tablespoons unsalted butter
- 1 tsp parsley

DIRECTIONS

1. **In a bowl toss shrimp with baking soda and salt, let it stand for a couple of minutes**
2. **In a skillet heat olive oil and add shrimp**
3. **Add garlic, red pepper flakes and cook for 1-2 minutes**

4. Add vermouth and cook for another 4-5 minutes
5. When ready remove from heat and serve

Serves: **2**

Prep Time: **5**   Minutes

Cook Time: **15**   Minutes

Total Time: **20**   Minutes

INGREDIENTS

- 2 tomatoes
- Olive oil
- ½ lb. eggplant
- ¼ cucumber
- 1 tablespoon lemon juice
- 1 tablespoon parsley
- ¼ head cabbage
- 2 tablespoons wine vinegar
- 2 pita bread
- ½ cup hummus
- ¼ tahini sauce
- 2 hard-boiled eggs

DIRECTIONS

1. **In a skillet fry eggplant slices until tender**

2. In a bowl add tomatoes, cucumber, parsley, lemon juice and season salad

3. In another bowl toss cabbage with vinegar

4. In each pita pocket add hummus, eggplant and drizzle tahini sauce

5. Top with eggs, tahini sauce and salad

Serves: **4**

Prep Time: **10** Minutes

Cook Time: **15** Minutes

Total Time: **25** Minutes

INGREDIENTS

- 2 tablespoons olive oil
- 2 carrots
- 1 head fennel
- 2 squash
- ¼ onion
- 1-inch ginger
- 1 cup white wine
- 2 cups water
- 2 parsley sprigs
- 2 tarragon sprigs
- 6 oz. salmon fillets
- 1 cup cherry tomatoes
- 1 scallion

DIRECTIONS

1. In a skillet heat olive oil, add fennel, squash, onion, ginger, carrot and cook until vegetables are soft

2. Add wine, water, parsley and cook for another 4-5 minutes

3. Season salmon fillets and place in the pan

4. Cook for 4-5 minutes per side or until is ready

5. Transfer salmon to a bowl, spoon tomatoes and scallion around salmon and serve

Serves: **4**

Prep Time: **5** Minutes

Cook Time: **15** Minutes

Total Time: **20** Minutes

INGREDIENTS

- 4 thick fish fillets
- ¼ cup all-purpose flour
- 1 egg
- 1 cup bread crumbs
- 2 tablespoons vegetables
- Lemon wedges

DIRECTIONS

1. In a dish add flour, egg, breadcrumbs in different dishes and set aside
2. Dip each fish fillet into the flour, egg and then bread crumbs bowl
3. Place each fish fillet in a heated skillet and cook for 4-5 minutes per side
4. When ready remove from pan and serve with lemon wedges

Serves: *4*

Prep Time: *10*   Minutes

Cook Time: *30*   Minutes

Total Time: *40*   Minutes

INGREDIENTS

- 2 tablespoons unsalted butter
- 1 leek
- 1 shallot
- 2 cloves garlic
- 2 bay leaves
- 1 cup white win
- 2 lb. mussels
- 2 tablespoons mayonnaise
- 1 tablespoon lemon zest
- 2 tablespoons parsley
- 1 sourdough bread

DIRECTIONS

1. In a saucepan melt butter, add leeks, garlic, bay leaves, shallot and cook until vegetables are soft

2. Bring to a boil, add mussels, and cook for 1-2 minutes

3. Transfer mussels to a bowl and cover

4. Whisk in remaining butter with mayonnaise and return mussels to pot

5. Add lemon juice, parsley lemon zest and stir to combine

Serves: **4**

Prep Time: **10**   Minutes

Cook Time: **20**   Minutes

Total Time: **30**   Minutes

INGREDIENTS

- 6 sprigs cilantro
- 2 cloves garlic
- 2 shallots
- ¼ tsp coriander seeds
- ¼ tsp red chili flakes
- 1 tsp zest
- 1 can coconut milk
- 1 tablespoon vegetable oil
- 1 tablespoon curry paste
- 1 tablespoon brown sugar
- 1 tablespoon fish sauce
- 2 lb. mussels

DIRECTIONS

1. In a bowl combine lime zest, cilantro stems, shallot, garlic, coriander seed, chili and salt
2. In a saucepan heat oil add, garlic, shallots, pounded paste and curry paste
3. Cook for 3-4 minutes, add coconut milk, sugar and fish sauce
4. Bring to a simmer and add mussels
5. Stir in lime juice, cilantro leaves and cook for a couple of more minutes
6. When ready remove from heat and serve

Serves: **4**

Prep Time: **10** Minutes

Cook Time: **20** Minutes

Total Time: **30** Minutes

INGREDIENTS

- 2 oz. egg noodles
- 4 oz. fraiche
- 1 egg
- 1 tsp cornstarch
- 1 tablespoon juice from 1 lemon
- 1 can tuna
- 1 cup peas
- ¼ cup parsley

DIRECTIONS

1. Place noodles in a saucepan with water and bring to a boil
2. In a bowl combine egg, crème fraiche and lemon juice, whisk well

3. When noodles are cooked add crème fraiche mixture to skillet and mix well

4. Add tuna, peas, parsley lemon juice and mix well

5. When ready remove from heat and serve

Serves: *4*

Prep Time: *10*   Minutes

Cook Time: *20*   Minutes

Total Time: *30*   Minutes

INGREDIENTS

- 1 lb. salmon fillets
- 1 onion
- ¼ dill fronds
- 1 tablespoon honey
- 1 tablespoon horseradish
- 1 tablespoon mustard
- 1 tablespoon olive oil
- 2 toasted split rolls
- 1 avocado

DIRECTIONS

1. Place salmon fillets in a blender and blend until smooth, transfer to a bowl, add onion, dill, honey, horseradish and mix well

2. Season with salt and pepper and form 4 patties

3. In a bowl combine mustard, honey, mayonnaise and dill

4. In a skillet heat oil add salmon patties and cook for 2-3 minutes per side

5. When ready remove from heat

6. Divided lettuce and onion between the buns

7. Place salmon patty on top and spoon mustard mixture and avocado slices

8. Serve when ready

Serves: *4*

Prep Time: *5*   Minutes

Cook Time: *10*   Minutes

Total Time: *15*   Minutes

INGREDIENTS

- 1 lb. sea scallops
- 1 tablespoon canola oil

DIRECTIONS

1. Season scallops and refrigerate for a couple of minutes
2. In a skillet heat oil, add scallops and cook for 1-2 minutes per side
3. When ready remove from heat and serve

Serves: *4*

Prep Time: *10* Minutes

Cook Time: *15* Minutes

Total Time: *25* Minutes

INGREDIENTS

- ¼ cup miso paste
- ¼ cup sake
- 1 tablespoon mirin
- 1 tsp soy sauce
- 1 tablespoon olive oil
- 4 black cod filets

DIRECTIONS

1. In a bowl combine miso, soy sauce, oil and sake
2. Rub mixture over cod fillets and let it marinade for 20-30 minutes
3. Adjust broiler and broil cod filets for 10-12 minutes
4. When fish is cook remove and serve

Serves: *4*

Prep Time: *10*   Minutes

Cook Time: *40*   Minutes

Total Time: *50*   Minutes

INGREDIENTS

- ¼ cup red miso
- ¼ cup sake
- 1 tablespoon soy sauce
- 1 tablespoon vegetable oil
- 4 salmon fillets

DIRECTIONS

1. In a bowl combine sake, oil, soy sauce and miso
2. Rub mixture over salmon fillets and marinade for 20-30 minutes
3. Preheat a broiler
4. Broil salmon for 5-10 minutes
5. When ready remove and serve

Serves: **2**

Prep Time: **10**   Minutes

Cook Time: **15**   Minutes

Total Time: **25**   Minutes

INGREDIENTS

- 1 lb. sweet potatoes
- 1 cup walnuts
- 1 tablespoon olive oil
- 1 cup water
- 1 tablespoon soy sauce
- 3 cups arugula

DIRECTIONS

1. Bake potatoes at 400 F until tender, remove and set aside
2. In a bowl drizzle, walnuts with olive oil and microwave for 2-3 minutes or until toasted
3. In a bowl combine all salad ingredients and mix well
4. Pour over soy sauce and serve

Serves: *4*
Prep Time: *10*   Minutes

Cook Time: *30*   Minutes

Total Time: *40*   Minutes

INGREDIENTS

- 1 oz. red potatoes
- 1 package green beans
- 2 eggs
- ½ cup tomatoes
- 2 tablespoons wine vinegar
- ¼ tsp salt
- ½ tsp pepper
- ½ tsp thyme
- ¼ cup olive oil
- 6 oz. tuna
- ¼ cup Kalamata olives

DIRECTIONS

1. In a bowl combine all ingredients together
2. Add salad dressing and serve

Serves: **4**

Prep Time: **10**   Minutes

Cook Time: **30**   Minutes

Total Time: **40**   Minutes

INGREDIENTS

- 2 tablespoons peanut oil
- ¼ onion
- 2 cloves garlic
- 1 tsp ginger
- 1 tsp cumin
- 1 tsp turmeric
- 1 tsp paprika
- ¼ red chili powder
- 1 can tomatoes
- 1 can coconut milk
- 1 lb. peeled shrimp
- 1 tablespoon cilantro

DIRECTIONS

1. In a skillet add onion and cook for 4-5 minutes

2. Add ginger, cumin, garlic, chili, paprika and cook on low heat

3. Pour the tomatoes, coconut milk and simmer for 10-12 minutes

4. Stir in shrimp, cilantro, and cook for 2-3 minutes

5. When ready remove and serve

Serves: *2*

Prep Time: *10*   Minutes

Cook Time: *25*   Minutes

Total Time: *35*   Minutes

INGREDIENTS

- 5 tablespoons butter
- ¼ onion
- 1 tablespoon all-purpose flour
- 1 tsp garlic powder
- 2 cups skim milk
- ¼ cup Romano cheese
- 1 cup green peas
- ¼ cup canned mushrooms
- 8 oz. salmon
- 1 package penne pasta

DIRECTIONS

1. Bring a pot with water to a boil
2. Add pasta and cook for 10-12 minutes

3. In a skillet melt butter, add onion and sauté until tender
4. Stir in garlic powder, flour, milk and cheese
5. Add mushrooms, peas and cook on low heat for 4-5 minutes
6. Toss in salmon and cook for another 2-3 minutes
7. When ready serve with cooked pasta

Serves: **2**

Prep Time: **10**   Minutes

Cook Time: **20**   Minutes

Total Time: **30**   Minutes

INGREDIENTS

- 4 oz. fillets tilapia
- ¼ cup all-purpose flour
- 1 tablespoon olive oil
- 2 tablespoons unsalted butter

DIRECTIONS

1. Season tilapia both sides with salt
2. Place each fillet into flour and coat
3. In a skillet heat olive oil and cook tilapia for 4-5 minutes per side
4. When ready remove from skillet and serve

Serves: 2
Prep Time: 5   Minutes

Cook Time: 5   Minutes

Total Time: 10   Minutes

INGREDIENTS

- 8 oz. sour cream
- ¼ adobo sauce
- 2 tablespoons lime juice
- 2 tsp lime zest
- ¼ tsp cumin
- ¼ tsp chili powder
- ¼ tsp seasoning

DIRECTIONS

1. In a bowl add all ingredients and blend well
2. Pour dressing in a serving cup
3. Serve when ready

Serves: **4**

Prep Time: **10** Minutes

Cook Time: **20** Minutes

Total Time: **30** Minutes

INGREDIENTS

- 8 leeks
- 1 lb. salmon slices
- 200g cheddar
- 2 oz. butter
- 2 oz. plain flour
- 400 ml milk
- 2 egg yolks
- 1 tsp mustard
- 1 tsp dill
- salt

DIRECTIONS

1. **In a pan bring water to a boil, add leeks and cook for 5-6 minutes**

2. When the leeks are cooked remove from the pan and place them in a baking dish

3. Add salmon over the leeks

4. In a pan melt butter, add flour and mix well

5. Whisk in milk and simmer for 2-3 minutes

6. Cook salmon fillets in mixture and set aside

7. In a bowl beat egg yolk, mustard, salt and pour over salmon

Serves: *1*
Prep Time: *10*   Minutes

Cook Time: *25*   Minutes

Total Time: *35*   Minutes

INGREDIENTS

- 100g king prawns
- 1 tablespoon olive oil
- 1 garlic clove
- 1 pinch chili flakes
- 1 carrot
- 8 cherry tomatoes
- 1 courgette
- 1 handful of basil leaves

DIRECTIONS

1. In a pan sauté garlic, add the prawns and sauté for another 2-3 minutes
2. Add carrots, cherry tomatoes, basil and courgette
3. Cook until the courgette is just heated
4. Season with pepper and lemon juice

Serves: *4*
Prep Time: *10* Minutes

Cook Time: *20* Minutes

Total Time: *30* Minutes

INGREDIENTS

- 1 lb. white fish
- 150g tiger prawns
- 3 oz. rapeseed oil
- 1 onion
- 1 fennel bulb
- 2 garlic cloves
- 1 tsp paprika
- 1 lb. tomatoes
- 800 ml fish stock
- parsley
- salt

DIRECTIONS

1. **In a pan add fennel, garlic, onions, paprika and stir to combine**

2. Add tomatoes, stock and bring to a boil, simmer for 10-12 minutes

3. Lower the heat, add fish and simmer for another 4-5 minutes

4. Add the tiger prawns and cook until the prawns are pink

5. Season with salt, parsley and serve

BANANA SMOOTHIE

Serves: *1*

Prep Time: *10*   Minutes

Cook Time: *30*   Minutes

Total Time: *40*   Minutes

INGREDIENTS

- 1 cup water
- 1 cup ice
- 1 banana
- ¼ cup cooked quinoa
- 1 tablespoons walnut
- 1 tsp flax oil
- ¼ tsp vanilla essence
- ¼ tsp cinnamon

DIRECTIONS

1. In a blender place all ingredients and blend until smooth
2. Pour smoothie in a glass and serve

Serves: *1*
Prep Time: **5**   Minutes

Cook Time: **5**   Minutes

Total Time: **10**   Minutes

INGREDIENTS

- **2 tsp Matcha**
- **¼ cup spinach**
- **½ avocado**
- **½ banana**
- **½ cup coconut water**
- **½ cup orange juice**

DIRECTIONS

1. **In a blender place all ingredients and blend until smooth**
2. **Pour smoothie in a glass and serve**

Serves: *1*
Prep Time: *5*   Minutes

Cook Time: *5*   Minutes

Total Time: *10*   Minutes

INGREDIENTS

- ½ cup water
- ¼ cup apple juice
- 1 tablespoon walnuts
- ¼ tsp cinnamon
- ¼ tsp vanilla extract
- ¼ cucumber
- 1 cup spinach
- 1 apple
- ½ avocado
- 1 cup ice

DIRECTIONS

1. **In a blender place all ingredients and blend until smooth**
2. **Pour smoothie in a glass and serve**

Serves: **1**

Prep Time: **5** Minutes

Cook Time: **5** Minutes

Total Time: **10** Minutes

INGREDIENTS

- 1 cup strawberries
- 2 tablespoons oats
- 1 tablespoon chia seed
- 1 tablespoon cashews
- 1 tsp apple cider vinegar
- 1 tsp lemon juice
- ¼ tsp vanilla

DIRECTIONS

1. **In a blender place all ingredients and blend until smooth**
2. **Pour smoothie in a glass and serve**

Serves: *1*

Prep Time: 5 Minutes

Cook Time: 5 Minutes

Total Time: *10* Minutes

INGREDIENTS

- 1 cucumber
- 1 cup spinach
- 1 cup ginger root
- 1 cup green tea
- 1 tsp lemon juice

DIRECTIONS

1. In a blender place all ingredients and blend until smooth
2. Pour smoothie in a glass and serve

Serves: *1*

Prep Time: *5* Minutes

Cook Time: *5* Minutes

Total Time: *10* Minutes

INGREDIENTS

- ½ cup water
- ¼ cup non-diary milk
- 2 cups spinach
- 1 banana
- 1 tablespoon hemp hearts
- 2 cups ice
- Mint (as much as needed)

DIRECTIONS

1. In a blender place all ingredients and blend until smooth
2. Pour smoothie in a glass and serve

Serves: *1*

Prep Time: 5   Minutes

Cook Time: 5   Minutes

Total Time: *10*   Minutes

INGREDIENTS

- 1 cucumber
- 1 apple
- ¼ cup raspberries
- 1 tablespoon chia seed
- ¼ cup water
- 1 apple
- 1 cup ice

DIRECTIONS

1. In a blender place all ingredients and blend until smooth
2. Pour smoothie in a glass and serve

Serves: *1*

Prep Time: *5* Minutes

Cook Time: *5* Minutes

Total Time: *10* Minutes

INGREDIENTS

- 1 cup non-diary milk
- ½ cup blueberries
- 1 tablespoon oats
- 1 tsp vanilla extract
- 1 cup ice

DIRECTIONS

1. In a blender place all ingredients and blend until smooth
2. Pour smoothie in a glass and serve

Serves: *1*

Prep Time: *5*   Minutes

Cook Time: *5*   Minutes

Total Time: *10*   Minutes

INGREDIENTS

- 1 cup non-diary milk
- ¼ cup raspberries
- 1 tablespoon lemon juice
- 1 tablespoon almond butter
- 1 tablespoon chia seeds
- 1 cup ice
- 1 cup water

DIRECTIONS

1. In a blender place all ingredients and blend until smooth
2. Pour smoothie in a glass and serve

Serves: **1**

Prep Time: **5** Minutes

Cook Time: **5** Minutes

Total Time: **10** Minutes

INGREDIENTS

- ¼ cup peach
- ¼ cup blueberries
- ¼ cup apple
- ¼ cup strawberries
- ¼ cup melon
- ¼ cup grapes
- 1 cup ice
- ¼ cup ice

DIRECTIONS

1. In a blender place all ingredients and blend until smooth
2. Pour smoothie in a glass and serve

Serves: *1*

Prep Time: *5*   Minutes

Cook Time: *5*   Minutes

Total Time: *10*   Minutes

INGREDIENTS

- 1 cup non-diary milk
- ¼ cup pumpkin
- ½ banana
- 1 tablespoon raisins
- ½ tsp cinnamon
- ¼ cup grapes
- 1 cup ice

DIRECTIONS

1. In a blender place all ingredients and blend until smooth
2. Pour smoothie in a glass and serve

Serves: *1*

Prep Time: *5*   Minutes

Cook Time: *5*   Minutes

Total Time: *10*   Minutes

INGREDIENTS

- 1 cup non-diary milk
- 2 cups spinach
- 1 banana
- 1 tablespoon flax seed
- 1 tablespoon almond butter
- 1 cup ice

DIRECTIONS

1. In a blender place all ingredients and blend until smooth
2. Pour smoothie in a glass and serve

Serves: *1*

Prep Time: *5* Minutes

Cook Time: *5* Minutes

Total Time: *10* Minutes

INGREDIENTS

- 1 cup non-diary milk
- 1 apple
- 1 tablespoon sunbutter
- 2 medjool dates
- ¼ tsp cinnamon
- 1 cup ice

DIRECTIONS

1. In a blender place all ingredients and blend until smooth
2. Pour smoothie in a glass and serve

Serves: *1*

Prep Time: **5**   Minutes

Cook Time: **5**   Minutes

Total Time: **10** Minutes

INGREDIENTS

- 1 tablespoon lime juice
- 1 cup non-diary milk
- 1 banana
- ¼ tsp vanilla extract
- 1 tablespoon sunflower butter
- 1 cup baby spinach
- 1 cup ice

DIRECTIONS

1. **In a blender place all ingredients and blend until smooth**
2. **Pour smoothie in a glass and serve**

Serves: *1*

Prep Time: *5* Minutes

Cook Time: *5* Minutes

Total Time: *10* Minutes

INGREDIENTS

- 1 cup non-diary milk
- 1 cup spinach
- ½ avocado
- 1 banana
- 1 cup ice

DIRECTIONS

1. In a blender place all ingredients and blend until smooth
2. Pour smoothie in a glass and serve

Serves: **1**

Prep Time: **5** Minutes

Cook Time: **5** Minutes

Total Time: **10** Minutes

INGREDIENTS

- 1 tablespoon vanilla essence
- 1 cup protein powder
- ½ cup blueberries
- ½ tsp maple extract
- 1 tsp flaxseed meal
- 1 cup ice

DIRECTIONS

1. In a blender place all ingredients and blend until smooth
2. Pour smoothie in a glass and serve

Serves: *1*

Prep Time: *5*   Minutes

Cook Time: *5*   Minutes

Total Time: *10*   Minutes

INGREDIENTS

- 1 peach
- 1 nectarine
- 1 cup cherries
- ½ cup non-diary milk
- ½ lime
- 1 cup ice

DIRECTIONS

1. In a blender place all ingredients and blend until smooth
2. Pour smoothie in a glass and serve

Serves: **1**

Prep Time: **5** Minutes

Cook Time: **5** Minutes

Total Time: **10** Minutes

INGREDIENTS

- 2 cups mango
- 1cup raspberries
- 1 cup non-diary milk
- 1 tablespoon ginger
- ½ lime
- 1 tablespoon coconut
- 1 cup protein powder
- 1 cup ice

DIRECTIONS

1. In a blender place all ingredients and blend until smooth
2. Pour smoothie in a glass and serve

Serves: *1*

Prep Time: *5* Minutes

Cook Time: *5* Minutes

Total Time: *10* Minutes

INGREDIENTS

- 1 banana
- 1 tsp cocoa powder
- 1 tablespoon flaxseed meal
- 1 dash stevia
- 1 cup spinach
- 1 cup strawberries
- 1 cup ice

DIRECTIONS

1. In a blender place all ingredients and blend until smooth
2. Pour smoothie in a glass and serve

Serves: *1*

Prep Time: **5**   Minutes

Cook Time: **5**   Minutes

Total Time: **10**   Minutes

INGREDIENTS

- 1 cup pomegranate juice
- 1 cup kale
- 1 cup blueberries
- 1 banana
- 1 cup ice

DIRECTIONS

1. In a blender place all ingredients and blend until smooth
2. Pour smoothie in a glass and serve

Printed in Great Britain
by Amazon

34948461R00066